COUPLES PRAYING TOGETHER

COUPLES PRAYING TOGETHER

Ways to Pray and Grow in Oneness

Charles and Sheila Michie

Empowerment Enterprise Publishing
TULSA, OKLAHOMA

Copyright © 2019 by Charles and Sheila Michie
All rights reserved. This book or any portion thereof may not be reproduced or used in any manner whatsoever without the express written permission of the publisher except for the use of brief quotations in a book review.

Printed in the United States of America
First Printing, 2019

ISBN 978-1-7331705-0-5

Images on pages 3, 22, 23, 25, 28, 34, 37, 43, 45, 51, 55, 58, 98
   by J. Soren Viuf, photographer. Used with permission.
Images on pages 33, 66, 84, 86, 91, 94, 100. Dreamstime.com.
   Used with permission.
Image on page 30. Pixabay. Used with permission.
Image on page 49. Artists Kathryn Grant & Kay Blanchard-Grell.
   Used with permission.
Image on page 67. Intercessors of the Lamb, Inc. Used with
   permission.

Empowerment Enterprise Publishing
Tulsa, Oklahoma
(918) 808-7383
email: CPT@letsempower.com
website: www.letsempower.com

02-02-2020

Dear Hayley & Chris,
　We hope this book will guide you together as you pray as a family.
　　　　Bob & Carole Scott

✝

2019

God's richest blessings be upon you.
　　　　Sheila & Mick

Table of Contents

Charles' Acknowledgment 8
Introduction 11
Sheila's Testimony 15
For Your Beloved 23
With Your Beloved 25
Traditional Prayers 29
Spontaneous Prayers and Praise 37
Using Scripture Verses 45
For Your Child(ren) 49
Over the Womb of a Pregnant Spouse/
Praying Over the Children Together 53
Over Each Other 55
For Healing 58
Intercessory Prayers 63
For Baptism in the Holy Spirit 67
In Tongues 74
Using Gifts of Knowledge and Prophecy 80
Spiritual Warfare Prayer 84
Contemplative Prayers 95
Various Other Types of Prayer 97
Closing 105
Notes 109

"I am my beloved's and my beloved is mine..."

~Song of Songs 6:3~

Charles' Acknowledgment

In reflecting on our journey in marriage and our hope for this project I first acknowledge Sheila. The concept for this couple's prayer booklet was entirely hers. Through it all, she kept the gift alive and nourished. Much of its creative material came from her, and with prayer and perseverance she bore its weight. It would never have materialized without her and the Holy Spirit. She deserves the credit. At best, I see myself as a contributing author and a beneficiary.

However, together, we can both acknowledge with deep gratitude that mysterious grace of our forebearers who—through joys and hardships—taught us faith and fidelity. My paternal grandparents are a heroic example. Solid in Christian faith, they were married 76 years! When asked how their marriage endured so long, they wryly replied, *"We just didn't know any better!"*

That line has such simple truth! No options may have been considered because divorce was as unacceptable as it was foreign. Sheila's parents remained married 60 years and mine 57. Not until their deaths did they part. Of course, enduring marriage and enjoying it are not the same. It's a man and a woman's journey in learning to die to oneself and discover together the reality of love.

With that understanding we've also been incredibly blessed with siblings who have taught us devotion and charity. Special friends also come to mind: Ted and Sherry Robinson, who in our first years of marriage reached out and showered us with Catholic community in Bartlesville, Oklahoma, and a prevailing affection for music ministry; Robert and Carole Scott and Ronald and Donna Wuerch, who have been extraordinary mentors and prayer partners, guiding us into mature discipleship; Philip and Maria Monhaut, whom we invited to experience a pilot of this content and from that experience we were inspired to proceed with the booklet.

Special thanks for assistance from: J. Soren Viuf for his time and the use of his photographs, Jean Yaeger with editing and Susan Coman with graphic design.

Finally, we are grateful for numerous priests who spiritually guided us, especially our Pastor, Reverend Elkin Gonzalez, Reverend James Conner, O.C.S.O., Reverend Thomas Carpender, and Reverend Jack Gleason.

Introduction

We are a Catholic Christian couple who take Jesus' words as Spirit and Life and the teachings of Catholic faith as the vanguard for our souls. Early in our marriage we recall a brief but critical search for the right Church to which we should commit our lives. It was ironically a Protestant evangelist with gifts of knowledge and prophecy who revealed to us that we have "a heart for the Catholic Church" and exhorted us to remain in it. That said, we embrace all good Christians as brothers and sisters.

This booklet is intended for all Christians: Catholic and non-Catholic, really for anyone who longs for purpose and fullness of life and therein desires to experience the Supreme Being as a loving and merciful God.

Satan has always come against marriage and family. But today, more intensely than ever, it's evident that the enemy seeks in countless ways to thrust evil into God's domestic Church and thus destroy society. We are blind if we do not recognize the obvious fragmentation and deterioration of human relationships rampant in our world. For this reason, we offer this booklet, far from exhaustive, as a toolbox to encourage and strengthen couples in experiencing a greater comfort, frequency, freedom and joy in praying, not only alone but more importantly together.

In this offering we are utterly human and quite aware of our past failings and tenacious shortcomings. But we are called to communicate the perspective that marriage and faithful prayer is a force, an overcoming triumphant force, with a divine aim and redeeming purpose! We firmly believe that when a husband and wife come humbly together before God in prayer, it may be one of the most powerful means of transforming the world and ushering in the kingdom of God on earth.

Of course, entering into marriage, couples must be wise, see themselves equally yoked, and be willing to sacrifice. Young men and women, far too early in life, yearn to experience some sense of affection, what on the surface appears as love. Founded on sand instead of rock, often relationships are terribly premature, lacking in personal discipline, trust, or any commitment. Becoming united only in a physical way, such relationships invariably end up regretted and, while other couples wait to be one with another for life, either the man or woman fail to see prayerful discernment is required.

In this booklet, therefore, we focus on the best aspects of married life and of our story, and it is intended for couples in various degrees and states of togetherness. Whether married, dating, courting, engaged, physically separated, and/or emotionally longing for reunion, it is vital to align the force of faith in advance and assess how well we are equipped with prayer. This scripture seems to speak to this:

"Or what king marching into battle would not first sit down and decide whether with ten thousand troops he can successfully oppose another king advancing upon him with twenty thousand troops? But if not, while he is still far away, he will send a delegation to ask for peace terms."
~Luke 14:31–32~

Sheila's Testimony

My dear brothers and sisters, not just the seven siblings with whom I was fortunate enough to be born into the same family, but all of you across this wide world...

As I begin writing, I am listening to Beethoven's 6th Pastoral Symphony, something I used to do often in my early 20s to get the creative juices flowing. That's the same desire I have now 40 years later. I could almost cry thinking that many decades have passed. I still feel that youth inside, the enthusiasm for life, and gratitude for peace and joy!

The Holy Spirit within us is so creative that He longs to inspire us with creative ideas to give glory to God and creative ways to become one with our beloved.

My precious husband, Charles, also known as "Mick" - is the beloved man given to me in marriage 39 years ago. He literally came singing into my life as a "fill-in" guitarist and has been serenading me ever since—no exaggeration. Since then we have faithfully journeyed together with an abundance of God's grace through the many years of our married life shared with Christ.

We marvel at this grace available to all, of course, through the sacraments of our Church, especially the Holy Eucharist, and in the Word of God that has helped us love the Lord, our God, with all our heart, being, strength and mind (Luke 10: 27) to the best of our ability. It strengthened and encouraged us through some very trying times.

As we reflect on our spiritual journey together as husband and wife, we recognize God's providence and how God prepared Mick and me before we became engaged. Some of this journey's details will be shared later in our own personal stories of how we experienced the Baptism in the Holy Spirit and first opened up to receive more of God's love, more of the Holy Spirit. That openness and an abiding belief there's always more, no matter what stage in life, have been essential for us in our capacity to pray and to pray often throughout our marriage.

When finally our footsteps crossed, God was without a doubt drawing us together. We were both 26, and quickly discerned that it was God's will for us to marry. Mick had recently become friends with a priest through whom he had begun exploring a vocation in the priesthood, and he had sensed a growing need to make a decisive commitment in his life. Mick recalls just four weeks before we met praying a specific, ardent prayer asking God to bring a woman into his life with whom he could make a lasting commitment, or else he would make application to the seminary, totally presuming of course a seminary would accept him.

I, on the other hand, had just finished praying a 54-day rosary novena for the "perfect" husband. I discovered the Lord knew far better than I did what I needed and what "perfect" meant. Of course, it didn't mean we would face life without hardships or suffering. Rather it meant through our union and various circumstances we would learn forgiveness, patience, and how to love unconditionally.

From the day I accepted his marriage proposal and we became fiancés, the good Lord led Mick and me into a relationship of hopeful, joyful prayer. During our courtship, until our wedding day, we faithfully prayed this beautiful prayer given to us by Mick's mother, Betty:

Lord Jesus,

To teach us to love one another you became one of us, taking as a tabernacle the body of Mary. You said: "Be one in each other, even as I and the Father are one."

You have desired that Mick and I should live in you as with a single life, like two branches of a single vine, which Your providence has entwined. Let our love pass through you, that it may realize a perfect union, not only of our hearts but also of our souls and that growing from day to day it may likewise increase our life in you.

Help us to bring to our home enough beauty, health, thrift, strength, purity and ideals to make it a model of the new world we wish to build with you and to give you priests perhaps, but certainly apostles.

With all of this, let us never forget that it is through us that your kingdom must be established on earth as in heaven. Have pity on all those youths and maidens whose hearts are wounded and whose dreams are broken. Guard the promises which have been made according to Your Spirit and may Your blessing soon give us to each other forever.

For a long time after marriage, we continued that prayer changing the last words to *"thank you for your blessing which has given us to each other forever."*

The wedding invitations were designed using the four seasons: *winter, spring, summer, autumn* with colorful images to match. So, no matter the season—cold, mild, or hot we were saying, "Yes!"

In fact our invitation was entitled: *"Our Love is an Endless Season"* and read: "God has been gracious. We have experienced love... in our parents, our families and friends and now a new love in each other. With abundant joy and an ardent desire to give this love its fullest expression we will be joined in marriage."

We were blessed indeed to have my own uncle, Fr. James Conner, O.C.S.O. presiding for the Nuptial Mass and a beautiful celebration of the sacrament of Holy Matrimony. We were inspired as well to write our own vows, which read:

I, ____, have chosen to marry you because I **am called to be one**

with you in Christ. *I will treasure my commitment of fidelity to you, and never betray that. I promise to hold you in your fragility as well as your strength. I will love you, honor you, forgive you, and celebrate with you. And I will be open to God's will in our life together.*

Truly our desire from day one has been this spiritual oneness. So holding each other in our fragility as well as our strength, we committed our wills that beautiful December day at the altar of Our Lord with many witnesses present.

Since then, there have been many things we've taken for granted, or perhaps haven't reflected on enough. As I reread our marriage vows I am more struck now than before that it begins with "I am called to be one with you in Christ." Those were words given to us by the Spirit of God and here we are almost 40 years later still awed by those words and these from John's Gospel:

"And I have given them the glory you gave me, so that they may be one, as we are one. I in them and you in me, that they may be brought to perfection as one..."
~John 17:22-23~

Both of us have our own deep personal relationship with the Lord. This has been essential. The three of us—Mick, the Lord, and I have been tightly woven together—three strands like the marriage plaque says hanging on our bedroom wall:

"Blessed is their lasting love, a seamless unity of heart and mind and spirit, shared not with two—but three." (Abbey Press)

Reflection questions:
- As a couple, what is your testimony or story of faith?
- What is the prayer of your heart–your inmost desire?
- How have you experienced grace (unmerited favor of God) in your relationship?
- In your life together for what are you most grateful?

Note

Ways for couples to pray: this list is what we were led to focus on for this guide; it is not an exhaustive or conclusive list. It is simply prayers we thought would help open up the hearts and minds of couples as they practice praying together.

+Praying

For Your Beloved

Before you ever begin learning to pray more with your beloved, it's important to pray **for** them for the graces and virtues they need to be open, receptive and cooperative in praying together and pray that any barriers be broken down that prevent them from receiving graces or practicing prayer. If they are already open and willing to pray together, just lift them up to the Lord in your own quiet time alone, whether it be at home, in the car, in church... asking that He would bless them abundantly and that the Holy Spirit would be poured out in greater measure upon their life.

Example: *Father, I pray you will bless _____ abundantly. Send the Holy Spirit upon him in greater measure. Give him everything he needs to be open to receive the many graces and blessings you*

have in store for him. May he experience your love and your presence in all that he does today...

Make it a daily habit to pray for one another, especially asking for the grace to grow in the capacity to pray with one another freely, joyfully and effectively.

> *"...pray one for another, that you may be healed. The fervent prayer of a righteous person is very powerful."*
> *~James 5:16~*

In praying for your beloved, you're bringing them on board with you as a trusting ally, and together as a couple our trust is in God. What a mighty force it is!

Reflection Questions:

- In what ways are you and your beloved allies in prayer?
- What graces might your beloved need for which you can pray?

+Praying

With Your Beloved

The main objective of this booklet is to pray as one with your beloved—to experience each other's mutual reliance on the Lord for every need and to invite the Lord into the various aspects of life. This can be at any time, about anything and virtually everything. Eventually, praying together becomes a common, even daily practice. This Gospel passage is the foundational scripture of this booklet:

> *"Again, [amen,] I say to you, if two of you agree on earth about anything for which they are to pray, it shall be granted to them by my heavenly Father. For where two or three have gathered together in my name, there I am in the midst of them."*
> *~Matthew 18:19-20~*

As we considered the power of two, we then thought of the power of three and remembered the gift of a plaque we received from Charles' parents. It says:

Marriage... A Unity of Three

"Blessed is the marriage that, from the very start, is built on selfless love, with Jesus at its heart. Blessed is the couple whose faith is strong and sure. With Jesus as their partner their devotion will endure. Blessed is the life they share—their laughter, joys and trials—for in the Lord their closeness will grow deeper all the while. Blessed is their lasting love, a seamless unity of heart and mind and spirit, shared not with two—but three." Abbey Press

The Holy Scriptures also refer to the power of three,

---

*"Where one alone may be overcome, two together can resist.
A three-ply cord is not easily broken."
~Ecclesiastes 4:12~*

There's an untapped force when two faithful and committed people come together and pray to God for the same intention. It's a force that's been too often suppressed and hidden from sight—like a buried treasure. Prayer enables couples to achieve amazing cooperation and spiritual oneness. At the same time, it deepens one's personal relationship with the Lord.

It should be remembered too that God always answers prayers. It may not be in exactly the way we expected or hoped in terms of timing, but He knows best and allows that which is most beneficial for our relationship and our salvation.

Reflection Questions:

- Are you experiencing the freedom and joy of praying together? If so, how? In what way?
- Can you identify two ways you can make prayer a daily practice in your relationship?

+Praying

Traditional Prayers

It may be helpful and most comfortable to use traditional prayers as a starting point. This is simply praying the well-known and centuries-old prayers such as the Our Father, Hail Mary, and Glory Be. It may be the best way to begin if you're not used to praying together as a couple. These beautiful prayers are not to be taken for granted. They are powerful!

One of his disciples said to Jesus, "Lord, teach us to pray…" He said to them,

> *"When you pray, say: Father, hallowed be your name, your kingdom come. Give us each day our daily bread and forgive us our sins for we ourselves forgive everyone in debt to us, and do not subject us to the final test."*
> *~Luke 11: 1-4~*

This, of course, is the perfect prayer since Jesus taught it. We can learn the model of prayer from it. Why? Consider how He begins—Our Father, not my Father.

Borrowing from a treatise on the Lord's Prayer by St. Cyprian, bishop and martyr, he states, "Above all, he who preaches peace and unity did not want us to pray by ourselves in private or for ourselves alone. We do not say 'My Father, who art in heaven,' nor 'Give me this day my daily bread.' It is not for himself alone that each person asks to be forgiven, not to be led into temptation, or to be delivered from evil..."

After addressing our Father, Jesus then gives praise and honor to Him in heaven— "hallowed be Thy name." As Cyprian further explains, "we are asking God that His name may be made holy in us." Then Jesus, in His prayer, focuses on earth where the Father desires His kingdom to come and His will to be done. God, our Father, is **counting on us** to cooperate and bring forth His kingdom on earth with "His help and protection" and through our prayerful actions.

So, an excellent starting point could be committing to pray one "Our Father" each morning before going separate ways— husband and/or wife to work and children to school, or as a family each evening after dinner, sharing what happened during each other's day. Or close with a "Glory Be" as a way of thanking God and giving Him the credit or glory for all the good things that happened or ways that you were enabled to do good.

One couple we know was inspired by another couple to imitate their practice of holding hands and praying one "Our Father" before drifting off to sleep.

One of our favorite ways of praying traditional prayers was inspired by some Filipino missionary brothers of the Alliance of Two Hearts from Delaware, whom we were transporting to our house for the enthronement of the Two Hearts of Jesus and Mary. As we left the rectory where they were staying, they asked us to join them in praying three Hail Mary's. Then when we stopped for something at a store along the way and after we got back on the road, they prayed three more. It was the same on the way back to the rectory after the enthronement. So, since 2002, we have kept that practice of praying three Hail Mary's before we drive anywhere—every leg of the trip. If we stop for gas, bathroom breaks, or whatever... when we get back on the road, we pray three more. This has helped us to integrate prayer into everything, not to mention it brings us a greater sense of safety and protection while on the road.

These five traditional Catholic prayers are beautiful to integrate into daily life:

Hail Mary

Hail Mary, full of grace, The Lord is with thee. Blessed art thou among women and blessed is the fruit of thy womb, Jesus. Holy Mary, Mother of God, pray for us sinners, now and at the hour of our death. Amen.

Glory Be

Glory Be to the Father and to the Son and to the Holy Spirit. As it was in the beginning is now and ever shall be world without end. Amen.

Grace Over Meals

Bless us, O Lord and these thy gifts, which we are about to receive from thy bounty, through Christ, our Lord. Amen.

Angel of God

(particularly good for children)

Angel of God, my guardian dear, to whom God love commits me here. Ever this night be at my side, to light and guard and rule and guide. Amen.

Morning Offering

O Jesus, through the Immaculate Heart of Mary, we offer you all our prayers, works, joys and sufferings of this day for the intentions of Your Sacred Heart, in union with the Holy Sacrifice of the Mass throughout the world, for the salvation of souls, in reparation for sin, the reunion of all Christians, and for the intentions of all my relatives and friends, and in particular for the intentions of the Holy Father. Amen.

We are reminded of a simple prayer that faculty and students pray each morning:

LaSallian Catholic School Prayer

"Let us remember we are in the holy presence of God."

Thus, as we slumber at night and rise in the morning all becomes prayer—unceasing prayer. Even our breaths can be offered and remind us that, *"God is with us."* (Matthew 1: 23) And, if you and I can see this, we will be blessed.

---

*"But blessed are your eyes,
because they see,
and your ears, because they hear."
~ Matthew 13:16~*

Reflection questions:

- Do you or your beloved have a favorite traditional prayer?
  If so, have you shared why it is your favorite?
- Could you and your beloved enter into the words of the prayer to discover a new and deeper meaning?

Example: Pray slowly the Hail Mary, which is derived from both the Annunciation of the Birth of Jesus and Visitation of Mary to Elizabeth found in the Gospel of Luke. Ask yourselves: what word or phrase of that prayer resonates most with you and why?

+Praying

Spontaneous Prayers and Praise

This is praying without any rote prayers or prepared script. It's turning spontaneously to the Lord and giving voice to the thoughts and feelings you both presently think or feel and allowing them to flow quite naturally from your heart. Spontaneous prayers can be applied in virtually every situation.

It's helpful to consider the often-used acronym, **ACTS,** with its letters standing for **A**doration, **C**ontrition, **T**hanksgiving and **S**upplication. Using this acronym's order, examples of spontaneous prayers might be:

Adoration

- *Lord, we **adore** you, we praise you, and we love you.*

Contrition

- *Have **mercy**, O God. Forgive us of our sin. We are truly sorry.*

Thanksgiving

- *We **thank** you, Lord, for your goodness, your kindness, your ever-lasting faithfulness.*

Supplication

- *Please, Lord, we beg you; **hear our plea**. Help us know what is the best way to handle this matter.*

St. Cyprian describes the striking story found in the Holy Scriptures about Shadrach, Meshach, and Abednego, who were cast into a fiery furnace by the strongest men in Nebuchadnezzar's army. (Daniel 3: 23-25)

> *"The three young men shut up in the furnace of fire observed this rule of prayer; united in the bond of the spirit they uttered together the same prayer. The witness of Holy Scripture describes this incident for us so that we might imitate them in our prayer. Then all three began to sing in unison, blessing God. Even*

though Christ had not yet taught them to pray, nevertheless, they spoke as with one voice. It is for this reason their prayer was persuasive and efficacious. For their simple and spiritual prayer of peace merited the presence of the Lord."

What strikes us is these three individual men "spoke as with one voice" and so "their prayer was persuasive and efficacious...[it] merited the presence of the Lord." These are words worth repeating—words worth pondering.

Praying spontaneously just takes some freedom and confidence in using our voice before the Lord. It helps to use the Psalms in scripture generally ascribed to David. They are full of his praise to God as well as expressions of all human emotion, and allow our feelings to flow from our heart.

---

*Enter his gates with thanksgiving,
and his courts with praise!
Give thanks to him, bless his name."
~Psalm 100:4~*

We suggest you lift up in prayer this praise as one voice. Just follow and proclaim the verses together. Imagine yourselves in the presence of the Lord and lift up your hearts to Him. Get a sense of what it feels like to let this spontaneous praise flow from your lips.

From Psalms:

"O Lord, our Lord, how awesome is your name..." Psalm 8:2

"I will praise you, Lord, with all my heart..." Ps 9:2

"I love you, Lord, my strength Ps 18:2

"Praised be the Lord..." Ps 18:4

"The Lord lives! Blessed be my rock!..." Ps 18:47

"Arise, Lord, in your power!.." Ps 21:14

"...You are God my savior..." Ps 25:5

"Lord, I love the house where you dwell..." Ps 26:8

"...Your face, Lord, do I seek!" Ps 27:8

"Blessed be the Lord..." Ps 28:6

"Give to the Lord the glory..." Ps 29:2

"I praise you, Lord..." Ps 30:2

"...Exalted be the Lord..." Ps 35:27

"How precious is your love, O God!..." Ps 36:8

"...The Lord be glorified." Ps 40:17

"...Lord, have mercy on me..." Ps 41:5

"Great is the Lord..." Ps 48:2

These are additional verses found in the first fifty Psalms that can be used:

"...You, Lord, are a shield around me..." Psalm 3:4

"I will delight and rejoice in you..." Ps 9:3

"I trust in your faithfulness..." Ps 13:6

"...You are my Lord..." Ps 16:2

"The heavens declare the glory of God..." Ps 19:2

"...I lift up my soul to my God..." Ps 25:1

"Good and upright is the Lord..." Ps 25:8

"Sing praise to the Lord..." Ps 30:5

"...forever will I give you thanks." Ps 30: 13

"How great is your goodness, Lord..." Ps 31:20

"For in God our hearts rejoice..." Ps 33:21

"Magnify the Lord with me..." Ps 34:4

"...You are my help and deliverer..." Ps 40:18

"Sing praise to God, sing praise..." Ps 47:7

Here's a shortened version of praise you might prefer:

> *We praise you, Lord. We bless you. We glorify you. We love you. You are wonderful. Holy, holy, holy, Lord. You alone are worthy. We adore you. Blessed be your name. We give you thanks. Thank you for your faithfulness. Glory and praise to your name. Jesus, Jesus, Jesus. We lift your name high. Bless the Lord, O my soul.*

Spontaneous prayer is often the caring, sincere, and wholehearted expression of what you may be feeling for or with your beloved. If you listen carefully to them you can simply use what they said and turn it into a prayer. Let's say your beloved tells you they experienced strife at work with a co-worker. After listening to them share details of the circumstance, ask if they'd like to pray about it together. If agreed, then take what has been said and pray it back.

Example: *Lord, I stand in agreement with _____ (my beloved) that things will be made right at his workplace. I pray that you will bring peace into this situation and enlighten him and the co-worker, by the power of your Spirit, with wisdom. Help them to learn and grow from this conflict. We trust in you to work this together for good...*

Reflection Activities:

- Describe your experience with spontaneous praise.
- Using your own words, write a spontaneous prayer of adoration.

+Praying

Using Scripture Verses

Incorporating words, phrases or verses of scripture you have read or that come to mind and praying them back in prayer can be a most powerful means of prayer. Why? Because you are standing on the very Word of God to bring your prayer intention to life. God honors this love for His Word. The Word does not go forth empty.

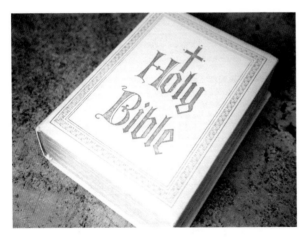

Wedding gift given to us by Sheila's uncle, Fr. Conner, that has a prominent place in our home.

"So shall my word be that goes forth from my mouth; It shall not return to me void, but shall do my will, achieving the end for which I sent it."
~Isaiah 55:11~

Let's look at the beautiful Word found in the Gospel of John:

> *And I have given them the glory you gave me, so that they may be one, as we are one. I in them and you in me, that they may be brought to perfection as one."*
> *~John 17:22-23~*

This is an example of how to pray this scripture back in prayer:

> *Lord, your word in the Gospel of John says you desire that we may be one as you and the Father are one. Make us one in you, Lord. You have given us this heart's desire. We turn to you, O God, and pray you bring our oneness to perfection, in Jesus' name, for your honor and glory. Amen!*

You can each think about and make a list of some of your most favorite scriptures. Then employ that verse, stand on that word—that promise—and use it in a prayer together for yourselves or someone else. It is the Word woven into a prayer like a tapestry. Here's one of our favorite scripture verses:

> *We know that all things work for good for those who love God, who are called according to his purpose."*
> *~Romans 8:28~*

Praying this verse back we might say,

> "Lord God, We love you and want your purposes to be fulfilled in our lives. We surrender the difficult situation we are facing into your hands and trust that you will work it all together for good as your Word promises."

And another favorite:

> *"For I know well the plans*
> *I have in mind for you,*
> *says the Lord,*
> *plans for your welfare, not for woe!*
> *Plans to give you a future full of hope."*
> *~ Jeremiah 29:11~*

We share this scripture verse often with incarcerated men and women to whom we minister at the city jail. We tell them no matter what we've done, how we've sinned, God's love is everlasting and He has good plans for our lives. It gives them hope for the future that we all need.

The main thing is praying from the heart and conversing with Jesus, who is the Word of God. He speaks in His Word and we listen and converse back with Him. This is a beautiful personal relationship and one that also plants the Word down deep in us.

Reflection Questions:

- What are your favorite scripture verses?
- When you read a particular verse you like, how might you shape that into a prayer for someone?
- Is there an implicit promise, admonition or exhortation in your verse? If so, what is it?

+Praying

For Your Child(ren)

Whenever you and your beloved have a specific intention, whether it be a longing, worry, concern, fear, hopes, dreams or heart's desires for your child(ren) that you may have been sharing about in conversation, or you just want to invoke protection or blessing on them, pray together as a couple for your child. Praying **with** your children is another way to pray. But this prayer, praying **for** your child, doesn't have to be in their presence. Adult children need their parents' prayers too, and not just young children.

Example: Our son is going to a conference in New York so we pray, *Lord, bless Joseph as he travels to New York for this conference. We pray you put a hedge of protection around him, surround him with the holy angels, and guide his every footstep.*

Stop and Ask: What is your heart's desire for your child? Maybe each of you has a different concern so both can be woven into your prayer.

Example: If a father is concerned about his son's lack of academic achievement and mother is concerned about his social life and lack of friends, you can pray something like this:

Lord, we lift up to you, _____, and pray that you bless him. Give him a greater desire to do his very best in school. Motivate him by the power of your spirit. Give him too, Lord, good and enriching friendships with some of his classmates. Give him courage to reach out to others, confidence while engaging in conversations and a stronger sense of belonging to his school community. We ask this for your greater honor and glory. Amen.

Here are other examples:

- As Nikki is preparing a list of colleges, please give her wisdom and discernment as she ponders the choices.
- John is trying out for Little League baseball. Help him do his best, but most importantly help him to accept whatever position his coach gives him.
- Carey is practicing for the upcoming recital. Give her the poise and grace needed to perform with her best ability.
- Our children are really yours, Lord, and we are simply stewards responsible for their care and upbringing. Please help us prepare them for the vocation in life to which you are calling them.

+Praying

Over the Womb of a Pregnant Spouse and Praying Over the Children Together

In 1977, I attended a healing conference at Oral Roberts University. There I learned the power of praying over a baby in the womb of a mother. When we married a couple of years later, we were fortunate to have this knowledge and daily prayed for our babies over my womb. It was beautiful to believe they could sense the love strongly as both mother and father (Charles and I) intentionally prayed together for them. Sometimes they would respond with a kick or a lot of movement.

Then when they were born, we prayed over them many times when they were asleep. Research shared at the healing conference indicated that children are more susceptible to prayer when in a sleep state. To learn more about this subject see: <u>Praying for Your Unborn Child</u> by Francis and Judith MacNutt.

So especially if one of our children had a difficult day, we would pray over them while sleeping at night, and the next day was often better. We attribute that to God's grace.

This was an original prayer composed by Sheila and prayed daily over our children when they were living at home:

May the precious blood of Jesus be upon you,
to protect, empower and purify you,
the holy archangels,
Michael, Gabriel and Raphael
surround and protect you,
the mantle of Mary's mercy be upon you,
and the glory of God be your rearguard.

Reflection Questions:

- What are your deepest hopes, dreams and aspirations for your child(ren)?
- How would you pray those into a prayer together?

+Praying
Over Each Other

This form of prayer is initiated in response to your beloved after they've shared something with you that may be troubling them. This requires listening carefully, some degree of vulnerability between the two of you when one may be feeling weak and needing to be humbly willing to receive prayer.

*"Have no anxiety at all, but in everything,
by prayer and petition, with thanksgiving,
make your requests known to God."
~Philippians 4:6~*

Perhaps they told you they don't feel well, are anxious about something, or they are concerned about a person or matter. It could be a number of different things. So, after listening to them, stop and ask if they'd like you to pray for them if they haven't already asked you to do that. If so, you simply place your hand on their shoulder and turn that concern, anxiety, lack of well-being, whatever it is, into a prayer. The point is you are bringing Christ Jesus into this matter.

Example: *Heavenly Father, _____ is giving a presentation today to a large group of people and she is feeling anxious. We stand in agreement together that the Holy Spirit will come and work through her. Come, Holy Spirit. I pray she will experience peace, joy and relaxation and we commit every detail of this presentation to you. May the people who hear this talk be blessed. We give you all the glory. In Jesus' name. Amen.*

Implicit in praying over your beloved is the recognition and understanding that oftentimes nothing—no advice or support—is as helpful in solving a problem or releasing a burden as invoking the Lord's intervention, calm presence and clear guidance. It is so important that your beloved understands that you heard them when you pray for them.

"Come to me, all you who labor and are burdened, and I will give you rest. Take my yoke upon you, and learn from me… For my yoke is easy, and my burden light."
~Matthew 11:28–30~

+Praying

For Healing

This prayer brings consolation, relief from pain and suffering, and restoration to wholeness. Short prayers of healing can be done at any time with family members who ask for prayer. We can take authority over sickness and pain and ask that the person be healed in the name of Jesus for His greater honor and glory.

Example: *Father, _____ is not feeling well. He has a headache and a lack of energy. Jesus, I ask that you come to him as his Divine Physician. Release your healing power in him. Touch him and make him well. Give him strength and take away that headache in Jesus' name. For your greater honor and glory restore him that he may continue to work to build your Kingdom.*

> *"...I, the Lord, am your healer."*
> *~Exodus 15:26~*

We are called as the disciples to proclaim the Gospel and to heal.

> *"He summoned the Twelve and gave them power and authority over all demons and to cure diseases, and he sent them to proclaim the kingdom of God and to heal [the sick.]"*
> *~Luke 9:1–2~*

God created us in such a way that we, as human beings, have need for human touch. Think of mothers and how quick they are to kiss a child's boo-boos and all of the sudden the child feels better. The pain seems to lessen. We think of the times we have prayed for others, placing a hand on their shoulder and how they have experienced peace. This is our Divine Physician working through us, His Body—the Body of Christ.

Jesus touched Bartimaeus' eyes and healed them of blindness, He touched the lepers, the paralyzed man, the woman with the hemorrhage, the epileptic boy and there are many other Gospel stories of how He healed people. He is alive and still healing.

We all have wounds that need to be healed in order to be made whole and Jesus longs to touch us and make us whole.

We witnessed something powerful at a national conference recently. There was a healing prayer night and Damian Stayne, an international Catholic preacher and teacher, was leading the session. As he began to call out different infirmities that the Lord was healing he asked the thousands of people in attendance to proclaim three times, "Jesus is alive!" And we did. Many were being healed during that time. Since then, we have added this powerful proclamation to our healing prayers for others. It's important for us to stop and ask ourselves, "Do you believe Jesus is alive?" As we ponder that we get a greater sense of his presence among us.

Another Catholic evangelist, Dr. Mary Healy, led a Healing and Evangelization Conference we attended recently. She taught a four-step healing prayer process. The steps include:

1. **Interview the person**—Example: Ask, *"How long have you had this? What do you want Jesus to heal you of? How has it affected your life?"* Keep it very short, very simple…if someone goes on and on, push the pause button. There is no time to counsel—we are here to be an instrument of the Lord.

2. **Pray with great expectancy**—Based on what that person has told you, pray and expect the Lord to do something. Avoid saying, *"If it be the Lord's will."* That's a cop-out for unbelief.

> *"...for I, the Lord, am your healer."*
> ~Exodus 15: 26~

Pray with great authority. Say, *"Lord, release your healing power in this person's life."*

Name the condition—and implore the Lord to heal it. Example: *"Lord, take away this pain. In your name I command it to leave."*

If you sense there is a contributing spiritual factor, be respectful...do you think there's anything on your conscience that may be hindering your healing like sin? unforgiveness? hurt? trauma? You can ask, *"Do you think there's anything on your heart that might need to be acknowledged...?"*

Example: Relationship with mother? The person may say, "No, I have not forgiven her...," So say a prayer for that... which may release them.

3. **Assess**--Stop and ask if they're aware of anything happening. If nothing, wrap up the prayer. If they do sense something, press into it.

4. **Thank the Lord** for what he's doing for you.
   Bless and encourage them. Say something like, "*You have stepped forward in courage and faith.*"

Mick and I are quick to pray over each other if we are not feeling well. At nighttime when sleeping, if one wakes up with an ache or pain, the other lays hands on them and prays for healing. Both of us have been healed many times through the years by the prayers of each other.

+Praying

Intercessory Prayers

It is important to pray together for others beyond our own personal needs. It could be for our Church, pastors, community, city or the world or any person in the world.

For a couple to engage in intercessory prayer, they have a good understanding of the end goal and purpose in life. We understand it is to live eternally in heaven. Jesus Christ, Son of the Living God, reigning in heaven, is now continually interceding on our behalf!

> *"It is God who acquits us. Who will condemn? It is Christ [Jesus] who died, rather, was raised who indeed intercedes for us. What will separate us from the love of Christ? Will anguish, or distress, or persecution, or famine, or nakedness, or peril, or the sword? ....No, in all these things we conquer overwhelmingly through him who loved us."*
> *~Romans 8:33-37~*

We therefore as children of God can exercise the extraordinary privilege of praying in cooperation with Jesus and with the heavenly host of saints, all drawing us and every person on earth so that we may be one with the Father.

It is this cooperation in the Spirit, this spiritual endeavor that any faithful couple can likewise join with Jesus—interceding on behalf of others, praying for their protection, welfare, peace, health, prosperity—anything that would be for the others' good and helpful in moving them into a deeper relationship with the Lord.

"Elijah was a human being like us; yet he prayed earnestly that it might not rain, and for three years and six months it did not rain upon the land. Then he prayed again, and the sky gave rain and the earth produced its fruit."
~James 5:17-18~

Our experience in intercessory prayer has been filled with wonder. Today when we hear a fire truck, ambulance, or police car siren it serves as a cue to intercede on behalf of the first responders and accident victims.

Example: *Lord, we pray you send holy angels to surround the person in need. Help them, Lord. Come to them. Give wisdom and knowledge to the first responders, nurses and doctors who care for them.*

A remarkable example is when Sheila awoke one night to the nearby alarm of many fire trucks realizing they seemed to stop in our neighborhood. We immediately interceded for the persons in that situation learning the next day that a family had narrowly escaped a blazing fire that had destroyed their home. Moreover, the man who owned the house was a well-known and respected non-denominational pastor and televangelist in Tulsa. Within a few days we shared this story of our intercession with the pastor, which was a witness of faith and drew us into a special bond.

We received a gracious personal letter in response from this couple saying among other things, "We are so grateful for the Body of Christ...We want to thank you for your personal touch in our lives during this time...The prayers you prayed and the letter you sent were very special to us." And then they prayed for God to multiply back to us in our life personally for the seeds of love shown to them.

All of this blessing came as a result of simply following a prompting of the Holy Spirit in the middle of the night. Sometimes the fruit of intercession may not be known, but still we trust the prayers go forth efficaciously.

+Praying

For Baptism in the Holy Spirit

"Let us discover, dear brothers and sisters, the beauty of being baptized in the Holy Spirit." Pope Emeritus Benedict XVI

As shared in the introduction of this booklet, we both received the grace of the Baptism in the Holy Spirit before we married. This is not the same baptism that we received when we were infants and reborn as sons and daughters of God. Praying for Baptism of the Holy Spirit, rather, is a conscious prayer to fully surrender to God and intentionally commit one's life to living according to His divine will. It is:

"A life-transforming experience of the love of God, the Father, poured into our heart by the Holy Spirit, received through a surrender to the Lordship of Jesus Christ. It brings alive sacramental baptism and confirmation, deepens communion with God and fellow Christians, enkindles evangelistic fervor and equips a person with charisms for service and mission." ICCRS Doctrinal Commission

In this section, Sheila shares her own personal witness:

"In my early 20s, I was somehow, and for some reason led to attend a charismatic conference at Holy Family Cathedral in downtown Tulsa. A young woman named Donna was one of the guest speakers, along with some members of the Benedictine Community from Pecos, New Mexico. I sat there that day thinking "I want what she has." She had an ability to teach and preach and a confident presence about being in front of a crowd. I felt somewhat shy and apprehensive of speaking in front of others.

So, on a break at the conference I asked a woman, who I knew was a leader in the charismatic renewal, if she would pray for me. I told her I wanted what that young lady had. She promptly did pray and another woman joined her. This is when I experienced a great outpouring of the Holy Spirit upon me and I began to speak in other tongues. You may have heard of that gift before—"speaking in tongues." The woman praying for me interpreted the tongues, and she said I was proclaiming the *Magnificat*. (Luke 1: 46-55)

This was my experience of being "baptized in the Holy Spirit" and when I opened up to an outpouring of God's love. It was truly an awakening into a deeper relationship with Jesus Christ, who we believe is "the way, the truth and the life." (John 14: 6) My life changed for the better then as I began to commit myself more fully to the Catholic Church and its sacraments. Though I am painfully aware of my shortcomings, I wanted from an early age, and still desire, to be a saint—that is the high calling for all of us. I fell short in those early years, and still fall short, but the grace of God continues to sustain me as I persevere to the final purpose of life—to spend all eternity with Him in Heaven."

Mick shares his own personal witness:

"Meanwhile, during the same period as Sheila's experience, I was working at Tulsa Boys Home, when a coworker invited me to a "revival" at St. Rita's Chapel on the campus of Cascia Hall Preparatory School. Reluctant and with no idea what to expect, I felt a prompting and went anyway. Upon arriving I witnessed Fr. Dario, a fiery Catholic priest, preaching from the pulpit and holding up his Bible declaring verbatim, "*This is our weapon against the enemy.*" I was so struck by the priest's claim for the Bible and his bold, animated fervor that when prayer teams assembled to pray for us in attendance, I went forward with a repentant heart and received prayer for the Baptism in the Holy Spirit. With this, I experienced a grace that shortly thereafter opened me to a new prayer language and a deep hunger to know God's Word and will.

This powerful experience awakened each of us individually to the Holy Spirit's activity in our lives and a deeper recognition of the gifts of the Spirit bestowed through the sacrament of Baptism and sealed when we were much younger through the sacrament of Confirmation. Indeed, through God's grace we had received those gifts, but this particular prayer opens and stirs up the gifts previously given. It gives us the power we need in the world to be ardent followers of Christ Jesus."

Jesus charged his apostles to wait for

" the promise of the Father
about which you have heard me speak;
for John baptized with water, but in a few days
you will be baptized with the Holy Spirit."
~Acts 1:4-5~

This grace is available to all….

> *"Ask and it will be given to you;*
> *seek and you will find;*
> *knock and the door will be opened to you."*
> *~Matthew 7:7~*

> *"Find your delight in the Lord who will give*
> *you your heart's desire."*
> *~Psalm 37:4~*

Praying together *in the Spirit* has been a relatively easy means of truly finding our delight in the Lord, the abundant life here and now, so much so we've considered it normal Christian living. Influenced also by Brother Lawrence in the book <u>The Practice of the Presence of God</u>, we learned how to pray at all times never thinking twice about it.

> *"With all prayer and supplication,*
> *pray at every opportunity in the Spirit…"*
> *~Ephesians 6:18~*

We have found that whatever we are doing around the house can be seen as a metaphor illustrating a lesson. For instance, while sharpening a knife in the kitchen and praying in tongues, we are reminded of God sharpening our conscience, or while wiping out the interior of an oven we ponder our own need for inner cleanliness and spontaneously proclaim, "Glory to God!"

We like to think of this practice of prayer as a Holy Spirit lifestyle—being open to the promptings of the Holy Spirit to pray constantly, and a Eucharistic lifestyle—one of continuously giving thanks to the Lord for all that He so generously gives to us.

---

*"How can I repay the Lord
for all the good done for me?
I will raise the cup of salvation
and call on the name of the Lord."
~Psalm 116:12–13~*

Pray: *Lord, we desire the promise of the Father. We humbly ask that you grant us this Baptism in your Holy Spirit. We need more of you. We open our hearts and surrender to you. We long to go forth to fulfill your command to love others and make disciples of all nations. Thank you for your goodness, Lord. We are yours. We long to do your will.*

+Praying

In Tongues

> *"Then there appeared to them tongues as of fire, which parted
> and came to rest on each of them.
> And they were all filled with
> the Holy Spirit
> and began to speak in different tongues, as
> the Spirit enabled them to proclaim."*
> *~Acts 2:3–4~*

As described in Acts, Jesus' disciples were praying in the upper room for the Holy Spirit to come, and indeed He came and filled them with new power to move out and speak in different tongues. Similarly, a new prayer language was experienced when we received the Baptism in the Holy Spirit, when faith-filled brothers and sisters in the Lord prayed for us to receive this gift. Praying this way was not a gift we earned or merited in any way, nor does the gift's use demonstrate one's holiness. Rather this gift shows the Father's incredible, lavish generosity, and His desire to help His sheep hear His Son's voice.

We received the gift in childlike humility, openness, and trust, simply desiring from the Father all the good gifts that He might desire to give us. Over the years we've learned the gift of tongues is endorsed by Mother Church, so we persevered in its use in daily life throughout our marriage. For us this supernatural gift has been a blessing, part of normal Christian living and we give thanks.

That said, we have also faced challenges. We are well aware most people do not pray in tongues and may see it as arcane and strange. It's hard to accept this gift perhaps because so little is known about it and it's rarely encouraged or offered by our clergy as a method of prayer. So, it remains misunderstood raising even suspicion among fellow Catholic Christians. Therefore, it may help to explain this gift.

To use an analogy, the gift of tongues may be likened to a water spigot where pure water is always available. When choosing to pray with tongues, it's as simple as choosing to turn the spigot on or not. The spigot will not turn on, unless one chooses to turn it on. The gift is exercised under the person's control in any given setting. In public settings, during Mass for instance, "the water's flow" may be turned down to a trickle to be discrete and out of respect for others. As St. Paul reminds us, "do not forbid speaking in tongues. But everything should be done in a fitting and orderly way" (1 Corinthians 14:39-40). However, in unrestricted settings, one may choose to allow "the water" to flow freely, unrestrained, perhaps intensely and joyfully. Regardless, it is always under the direction by the one praying. It's also in accordance to the Holy Spirit's purpose and leading.

In that regard, to learn to pray in this way requires our spirits to be submitted to and freely cooperating with the Lord's Spirit. It helps to imagine or recall yourself as a child, if you can, perhaps at the ages 3, 4, or 5. You may be playing in the sandbox pouring sand through your hand, or walking alone in the yard along a fence with a stick in your hand hearing the rapping of your stick on the pickets. In amusement and sheer delight you find yourself in reverie humming then uttering a song, or actually just a flow of syllables. It flowed from your lips because you were just in God's creation, in awe, serene and joyful. Your spirit seems to be communing with God's. Here, we momentarily break out from what seems logical, for logic can often impede our receptivity to the wonder of this gift and its practice. The analytical mind is a good and natural gift as well, but it often diminishes one's capacity and freedom in using tongues.

> *"Trust in the Lord with all your heart,*
> *on your own intelligence rely not;*
> *in all your ways be mindful of him,*
> *and he will make straight your paths."*
> *~Proverbs 3:5–6~*

A childlike trust and an utter dependence on God's wisdom seem to be requisites in receiving this gift. Once received it helps pave the way for uniting our spirit with God's Spirit, for clearing a path for the Lord to speak clearly into our hearts and minds. The Spirit wants to help particularly considering we are human and, sometimes, we don't know what to say or do, or we have no idea how best to pray.

> *"Then Spirit too comes to the aid of our weakness; for we do not know how to pray as we ought, but the Spirit itself intercedes with inexpressible groanings. And the one who searches hearts knows what is the intention of the Spirit, because it intercedes for the holy ones according to God's will."*
> *~Romans 8: 26–27~*

It should be remembered God's gift of tongues is to be used for His service, which encompasses all of life. So throughout our marriage we have relied upon this gift in countless situations. We have found praying in tongues, whether alone or together, is helpful for our personal relationship with the Lord. The Spirit helps us enter intimately into His courts with thanks and jubilation, to adore and praise His holy name when no words can be expressed. Such is the case during the Holy Sacrifice of the Mass where we have learned to speak our prayer language inaudibly allowing us to enter more fully and consciously into divine worship.

Again, so often we do not know how to pray, but the Spirit does. So we may pray for the Lord to give us needed insight and understanding in a given matter, to help us discern some practical course of action and to know more clearly the Lord's will for us. For instance, before choosing and buying our home, we used our prayer language to seek clarity and discern the best course of action.

On a far larger scale we live in a world fraught with sin and extraordinary suffering, a world in which we are called to militate. We may utter unintelligible groans of sorrow and compassion for terrible situations that defy explanation. As well the Spirit's gift provides an immense source of comfort and consolation as when Sheila received the phone call that her father had a life-threatening heart attack. Setting down the phone we immediately prayed in tongues pleading for mercy and healing, trusting that God heard our prayer and would answer it, according to His will.

If willing, we encourage you and your beloved to accept this beautiful gift of the Spirit and seek someone with experience to pray for your reception. If you desire this gift, ask for it. You and your beloved will be nothing short of blessed.

Example: *Father, with childlike faith and openness, I ask for this gift of tongues that I may be able to expand my prayer language. I give you my breath and the sound of my voice. Please form it into your holy language.*

+Praying

Using Gifts of Knowledge and Prophecy

Praying in this way helps one to learn to listen better for the Lord's still small voice and to recognize and discern supernatural words of knowledge that reveal, to the person being prayed for, a sense of God's great love for them. Words of prophecy can also be given in prayer that encourage and give hope for their life.

Our friend and mentor, Carole Scott, taught us to pray this way. While praying for someone, you simply ask these two questions:

- Lord, how much do you love this person?
- What is your desire for this person?

Now, pause for a moment or two and listen with your heart. Whatever loving word you hear or sense you have, share it with your beloved. Make sure it is loving. We avoid saying anything that would cause fear or confusion or discouragement. For instance, if you sense a lack of faith or resistance while praying for someone, pray for an increase of faith and openness and not anything that mentions lack of faith. In other words, make it positive and not something negative that would discourage or annoy the person.

Example: _____, *when I pray for you asking how much the Lord loves you and what His concern is for you, I get a sense that He is saying: "I have loved you with an everlasting love."*
(Jer 31: 3)

> *"And behold,
> I am with you always..."*
> *~Matthew 28:20~*

Helpful hints for gift of knowledge:
- Pray quietly until you get a sense of what the Spirit is saying...
- Pay attention to any word, scripture verse, image, or song that comes to your mind.
- You don't have to say everything you hear or see. Be discerning.
- Share that with the person and ask if it means something to them.

When we speak of prophetic words, this is not predicting the future. Only God knows what lies ahead in someone's life. Rather, it is communicating something that brings hope to the person.

Example: *"For I know well the plans I have in mind for you, says the Lord, plans for your welfare, not for woe! Plans to give you future full of hope."* (Jer 29:11)

Helpful hints for gift of prophecy:

- Ask the Lord, "What is your hope for their future?"
- Pray quietly until you get a sense of what the Spirit is saying…
- Pay attention again to any word, scripture verse, image, or song that comes to your mind.
- Again share with the person what came to you.

As a couple, we go to a private peaceful place. You can go any place where you feel you can pray. It may be next to a stream or flowing river. We love to go to an adoration chapel where the Lord is present in the Blessed Sacrament to ask Him to reveal to us His direction in a time of decision-making and to also give us a confirmation.

Example: *Lord, please reveal to us a word or idea, scripture or image of what you want to impress upon us about this decision. We commit this decision to you and pray for the grace to hear your voice, sense your presence and know what next step to take. We desire your holy will, Lord.*

We just sit quietly in the presence of the Lord and listen for His voice. We take a pen and paper so we can write down what comes to us. It is powerful when we both receive a similar word or sense of direction. This is a confirmation. After we leave the chapel, then we discuss what each of us has received from the Lord during that intimate time.

+Praying

Spiritual Warfare Prayer

From the beginning, too, we set out into our marriage mindful that we needed to be steeped in the scriptures because we would be fighting a spiritual battle. We were resolved and ready to fight the good fight for love, and to do so in every season.

"Fight the good fight of the faith; take hold of the eternal life to which you were called..."
~1 Timothy 6:12~

Aware that the reality of battles in life and in relationships are often spiritual warfare, this prayer girds us and equips us with the power to gain victory, not against flesh and blood, but against an enemy that seeks to divide and destroy. Spiritual warfare prayer recognizes that we are more than conquerors through Christ's love.

> *"... in all these things we are more than conquerors*
> *through him who loved us."*
> *~Romans 8:37~*

So in Jesus' name, the name above all names, we recognize and remember our true identity that, as adopted sons and daughters of God Almighty, and as priest, prophet and king by virtue of our baptism, we can take authority over evil spirits. It's praying like Paul in Ephesians 6:10–18 teaches us—to "put on the armor of God... to stand firm" when temptation or very trying times come our way.

We encourage you to learn more about how to put on the "armor of God" by reading Ephesians, Chapter 6:13–18, the last verse of which bears out the need for constant prayer:

> *"With all prayer and supplication, pray at every opportunity*
> *in the Spirit. To that end, be watchful*
> *with all perseverance and supplication..."*
> *~Ephesians 6:18~*

Spiritual battle can intensify if we have unforgiveness in our heart towards someone or unrepented sin. It can cause a hole in our spiritual armor and make it easier for us to give in to the devil's temptations. So, it is of utmost importance to forgive those who have hurt or offended us, with the help of God's grace, and to confess our sins. As the Our Father says, *"and forgive us our sins for we ourselves forgive everyone in debt to us,..."* (Luke 11:4)

In any committed relationship, conflicts will naturally arise over a wide range of issues in varying degrees of intensity and the need for forgiveness is going to be present and perhaps frequent. Throughout our marriage of 39 years we have had to ask forgiveness on many occasions. Jesus' admonition in the following scripture rings true for us and brings us understanding of our humanity:

> *"Then Peter approaching asked him, "Lord, if my brother sins against me, how often must I forgive him...as many as seven times?" Jesus answered, "I say to you, not seven times but seventy-seven times."*
> *~Matthew 18:21-22~*

One of the hardest things to do in a relationship is to say, "I am wrong," and ask for forgiveness. If we don't forgive, if we are not willing to be honest and admit our wrong-doings and ask for forgiveness, grudges can be stored for years, and become bitter roots. We need to pray for the grace of forgiveness so that we can keep an open heart.

The issues involved in disagreements may be superficial, and oftentimes a simple apology is all that's needed by one or the other. Other conflicts reveal hidden issues, far deeper areas of the heart, that need to be gently explored with compassion and love. When one of us is vulnerable and revealing weaknesses, we've learned we need to be listening attentively and responding with acceptance, care, and kindness.

"Above all, let your love for one another be intense, because love covers a multitude of sins."
~Peter 4:8~

Forgiveness may be the most critical requirement if two people are going to mature, become one, and through their union eventually bear fruit. It requires a willingness to risk and become vulnerable. Both have to admit that the Holy Spirit could be speaking through their beloved. What's revealed can be a surprise, a gift that can open a couple to new horizons in their relationship.

All human beings face temptations by the devil, even Jesus did. So when we sense temptation, how can we practically resist? Let's look and meditate on Jesus' example and how he persevered through the devil's fierce attack in the desert:

"Then Jesus was led by the Spirit into the desert to be tempted by the devil. He fasted for forty days and forty nights, and afterwards he was hungry. The tempter approached and said to him, 'If you are the Son of God, command that these stones become loaves of bread.' He said in reply, 'It is written: One does

not live by bread alone, but by every word that comes from the mouth of God.' Then the devil took him to the holy city and made him stand on the parapet of the temple, and said to him, 'If you are the Son of God, throw yourself down. For it is written: He will command his angels concerning you, and with their hands they will support you, lest you dash your foot against a stone.' Jesus answered him, 'Again it is written, You shall not put the Lord your God to the test.' Then the devil took him to a very high mountain and showed him all the kingdoms of the world in their magnificence, and he said to him, 'All these I shall give to you, if you prostrate yourself and worship me.' At this, Jesus said to him, 'Get away, Satan! It is written: The Lord, your God, shall you worship and him alone shall you serve.' Then the devil left him, and behold, angels came and ministered to him."

~ Matthew 4:1-1~

These eleven verses have been included in their entirety because it clearly demonstrates that Jesus fought against Satan's temptations with the Word of God and was victorious. It demonstrates that Jesus was prepared to handle Satan's temptations because He had previously been in prayer and fasting. Jesus in His divine wisdom cut through Satan's pride, arrogance and presumption in his very attempt to command the Lord.

Through the prayers suggested in this booklet, couples can more firmly stand against the attacks and divisiveness of the enemy.

For Catholic Christians, Mary, the Mother of God, is venerated. She holds the most prominent place in the communion of saints, and for that reason her intercession is powerful. Mary was given to all the Church at the foot of the cross when Jesus said to John, "Behold your mother." John was representing the whole Church.

We find ourselves turning to our Heavenly Mother through this prayer when things get most difficult:

Memorare

Remember, O Most Gracious Virgin Mary, that never was it known, that anyone who fled to thy protection, implored thy help, or sought thy intercession was left unaided. Inspired with this confidence, we fly to thee, O Virgin of Virgins, our Mother. To thee do we come, before we kneel, sinful and sorrowful. O Mother of the Word Incarnate, despise not our petitions, but in thy mercy hear and answer us.

Another most powerful prayer when faced with spiritual warfare, was composed by Pope Leo XIII:

Prayer to St. Michael, the Archangel

St. Michael, the Archangel, defend us in this day of battle. Be our protection against the wickedness and snares of the devil. May God rebuke him we humbly pray and do thou, O Prince of the Heavenly Host, by the power of God cast into Hell, Satan and all the evil spirits who prowl through the world seeking the ruin of souls. Amen.

We can take authority over the enemy because we have Jesus within us, and He is the authority over all. We can one-by-one bind any spirit, for example, of jealousy, frustration, discouragement, despair, anxiety, resentment, fear, confusion all in the holy name of Jesus and by the power of His blood. We can then ask for an outpouring of the Spirit we need--- peace if anxious, courage if fearful, knowledge if confused, counsel if lacking direction, confidence if in doubt, forgiveness if bitter, hope if despairing, faith if unbelieving, and others.

When Sheila has felt tempted, I have renounced that spirit and prayed for her to be filled with courage, fortitude and strength instead.

Often we have prayed for others who have been fearful or afraid and we remind them of this scripture verse:

> *"For God did not give us a spirit of cowardice but rather of power and love and self-control."*
> *~2 Tim 1:7~*

And we pray, "In the name of Jesus, I bind the spirit of fear." Then we ask the Holy Spirit to come and fill them with courage and an increase of power, love and self-control.

We must remember the Lord came to give us life and give it in abundance and the devil wants just the opposite.

> "The thief comes only to steal
> and kill and destroy;
> I came that they may have life,
> and have it abundantly. "
> ~John 10:10~

Pray: *Heavenly Father, we are aware there is an enemy who seeks to rob, steal and destroy. We desire your will and the abundant life you have promised found only in your Son. Help us to stand strong, to stand firm against the tactics of the devil. We pray that you give us all the graces we need to be victorious. In Jesus' name, Amen!*

+Praying

Contemplative Prayers

This is a more silent prayer of resting in the Lord, soaking in His presence, just being content to take time with Him and know that this invitation to rest leads us into a more intimate union with Him.

This is a way of responding to the Lord—letting Him know His presence is enough. We don't need to say a word. We let our thoughts pass through our minds. We can't control what comes into our mind but we can choose to entertain thoughts, so we choose not to do that. Let thoughts float through without resistance.

Example: We have been in a prayer group for many years that integrates contemplative prayer. We start with a theme, usually a song or scripture verse that we use as a focus. We briefly pray together and ask the Holy Spirit to come and enlighten us. We remember where two or three are gathered in his name, He is in our midst. Then we take quiet time to sink deeply into His presence, listening...

> *"Put out into deep water and lower your nets for a catch."*
> *~Luke 5:4~*

We pay attention to breath and relax as much as possible. We have a pen and paper where we can write the things that come to mind. We allow at least 10 minutes to pass before we share what the Holy Spirit brought to our mind during that time. Then we repeat another round of that same process asking the Lord to take us deeper in understanding what He is communicating to us and inviting us to do.

Thomas Merton's book <u>New Seeds of Contemplation</u> was life-changing for me. I read it during those early 20s years when I was really searching and seeking something more and it changed my life. It caused me to understand the difference between my will and God's will and I chose His will by sheer grace.

Pray: *"Speak Lord, your servant is listening." (1 Sam 3:9) You have the words of everlasting life. I offer you my breath, my thoughts, my emotions and ask that you will quiet all of them while I sit here and relax and do nothing else but imagine myself in your presence.*

+Praying

Various Other Types of Prayer

We want to briefly share with you some other meaningful prayers we have prayed through the years. The following prayers may be enjoyed as a couple or in one's individual prayer time.

+Lectio Divina—If you want to be enlightened about the scriptures, this is a method that teaches one how to go deeper in the Word. Lectio Divina is a four-fold process that includes:

Lectio (Reading)—Read the Word and focus on the facts of what, when, where, who…more factual things.

Meditatio (Meditation)—Read the Word again and pay attention to what word or phrase resonates with you, jumps out at you. Trust that word or phrase is something the Spirit is wanting you to ponder so that you can understand more about what God is speaking to your heart. In reading, be attentive, repetitive, and selective. One phrase or word can be charged with great wisdom and divine meaning.

Oratio (Prayer)—After pondering, take your reflections to prayer. Invite the Lord in with you. Express to Him what struck you, what you think and how you feel about it. Ask for any graces you think you may need to live out that Word more fully in your life each day.

Contemplatio (Contemplation) Now take time to just rest in that fresh revelation of God's Word. Allow yourself to soak in His presence. And let gratitude rise in your heart for that sweet time of serene abandonment in the gentle hands of the Father.

+Liturgy of the Hours—We are Benedictine Oblates so we love to pray this way in the mornings as often as we can. We're wonderfully uplifted and refreshed when we do. This way of praying, also called the Divine Office, was begun by the Desert Fathers and developed by St. Benedict. Clergy and religious throughout the world pray these traditional

and standardized prayers day and night. They are filled with psalms, spiritual readings, hymns, and prayers. Sheila was exposed to Liturgy of the Hours at an early age when her parents took her and her siblings to the Abbey of Gethsemani in Kentucky where her uncle, Fr. Conner, resides and the prayers are still being prayed around the hours as they have been there for 170 years now. Just to clarify, being an Oblate means we are affiliated with a Benedictine monastic community. We have offered our lives to God and to practicing the Rule of St. Benedict as much as we can in our state of life. That's something you can search in different sources if you want to know more.

+Novenas—This refers to prayers elevated for a specific intention during nine consecutive days. I shared with you that I prayed a 54-day rosary novena for the "perfect" husband. That means I prayed six novenas in a row. Other novenas that are often prayed by Catholic Christians are to the saints who are now in heaven interceding for us with the Lord. We begin the novena nine days before a saint's feast day and ask for their intercession. This can also be done for other Feast Days and Solemnities. We highly recommend the Divine Mercy novena. It begins on Good Friday (before Easter Sunday) since the Divine Mercy Feast is the first Sunday after Easter. We encourage you to search and learn more. **Pray More Novenas** is a good internet resource that helps one stay connected with novenas according to the Catholic liturgical calendar.

+Sunday Readings—We have found it meaningful to take time to read in advance and reflect on the upcoming Gospel that we will hear at Church on Sunday. We simply like to share what means most to each of us in the reading and how we sense the Lord is inviting us to be, or what he may be calling us to do. The same approach as Lectio Divina can be applied here. This reflection helps to prepare our hearts for the Sunday Liturgy of the Word.

+Rosary—Praying the rosary has brought us many graces through the years. It is powerful and how our Heavenly Mother has asked us to pray to have peace in our world. It also brings much peace into people's souls, homes, and communities. When using rosary beads and praying in this way, we meditate upon one of the four mysteries of the rosary—either Joyful (Jesus' early years), Luminous (His mission), Sorrowful (His passion & death) or Glorious (After His death, i.e., resurrection, ascension…). All of these mysteries focus on some aspect of the life of Jesus. We teach this to the inmates we work with in the Tulsa County Jail. It's edifying to see how much it means to them. It means a great deal to us too.

+Adoration together—Going to adoration together as a couple means finding a Catholic chapel where the Blessed Sacrament is exposed in what is called a monstrance. As Catholics, we believe in the real presence of Jesus in the consecrated host. This is the best place for contemplative prayer, a place where we can sit together silently in the presence of Our Lord and listen to His voice. If you are not Catholic, you are still welcome to come to our adoration chapels. You can search and find the location of an adoration chapel in whatever place you reside or visit. You can also make a special place in your home for prayer, or outside somewhere where you can simply be quiet and admire the gift of God's creation.

+Blessing of a Home—This is an intentional prayer over the place where you reside. Over the years, we have invited priests to come to our home for a house blessing. They usually come with a prayer book with a house blessing in it. At other times we have provided it. Our favorite blessing is done with exorcised salt and holy water. After praying, the priest has sprinkled holy water in all rooms inside and around the exterior of our home and property as well. This is a way of setting apart our home for the Lord's purposes. It has also offered us a greater sense of protection of our property.

+Dedication of Rooms to the Saints—One Christmas after our children left to go back home (they lived out of state at the time) we were feeling a little sad, so Charles was inspired with the idea of naming each room after a saint. He thought it would bring us some consolation and it did. So as a couple or family, you might consider naming the rooms of your home after a saint. It can be a fun and meaningful activity with children. Think of the saints you love and are drawn to and name rooms after them. Each room in our home has a picture of the saint—often a simple holy card placed above the doorway.

For instance, just to share a few of our saints in our home, the great room is named after Pope St. John Paul II, our guest room after St. Benedict known for the charism of hospitality, and our yard is dedicated to St. Francis of Assisi. After all rooms are named you can pray your own daily litany of the saints of your home. So our litany begins with St. Michael, the Archangel, pray for us, St. Ignatius of Loyola, pray for us, St. Catherine of Siena, pray for us… and so on and so forth. It's wonderful to sense the heavenly cloud of witnesses near.

+Feast of the Epiphany House Blessing—This feast day falls twelve days after Christmas Day. We have enjoyed renewing an annual house blessing at the beginning of a new calendar year. We do this by praying the Epiphany house blessing and writing certain symbols above our doorways using blessed chalk. The letters are the initials of the three Magi and also the abbreviation of the Latin words *Christus mansionem benedicat m*eaning "May Christ Bless the House." It looks like this: 20 + C + M + B + 19. The + symbolizes the cross and 2019 the year.

Closing

In closing we encourage you, be confident, open and receptive. On Catholic radio we frequently hear this announced, *"Be a saint! What else is there?"* No doubt, that's the high calling! This is the inspiration that keeps us persevering to the end. The world desperately needs saints—people who are heroic in loving and serving the Lord and others—particularly married or engaged couples who recognize and embrace their humanity yet believe in, and are always open to, receiving the graces God extends, whether circumstances be good or bad, rich or poor, sickness or in health.

In striving to be better and to become holy, may all our efforts be grounded in a wonderful life of prayer! Then all our works, joys and sufferings are aligned with God's will, through His power, and for His glory. Be confident too that God in His wisdom knows best how to bring about such sanctification. For two becoming one flesh is a mystery and a miracle. Be open and receptive to mysteries and miracles.

It is truly our hearts' desire that this booklet bears fruit, especially the grace for couples to grow in their capacity to pray daily, faithfully, freely and joyfully…to know the source of perfect love given in one another and for service to one another.

---

*"Every good and perfect gift
is from above..."*
~James 1:17~

---

*"As generous distributors of
God's manifold grace,
put your gifts
at the service of one another,
each in the measure
he has received."*
~1 Peter 4:10~

And this, dearly beloved, is our final prayer for you:

"The Lord bless you and keep you;
the Lord make his face to shine upon you,
and be gracious to you;
the Lord lift up his countenance upon you,
and give you peace."
~Numbers 6:24-26~

NOTES

Table of Contents
Song of Songs 6:31   The Didache Bible

Introduction

Luke 14:31-32   New American Bible/St. Joseph's Edition

Sheila's Testimony

Luke 10:27   New American Bible/St. Joseph's Edition

John 17:22-23   New American Bible/St. Joseph's Edition

Wedding invitation inscription   Unknown

"Blessed is their lasting love…"   Abbey Press

For Your Beloved

James 5:16   New American Bible/St. Joseph's Edition

With Your Beloved

Matthew 18:19-20   New American Bible/St. Joseph's Edition

Marriage...A Unity of Three, "Blessed is the Marriage..." Abbey Press

Ecclesiastes 4:12   The Catholic Study Bible

Traditional Prayers

Luke 11:1-4   New American Bible/St. Joseph's Edition

St. Cyprian of Carthage Treatise IV on the Lord's Prayer

Matthew 1:23   New American Bible/St. Joseph's Edition

Matthew 13:16   New American Bible/St. Joseph's Edition

Spontaneous Prayers and Praise

ACTS acronym, not the same as acronym used for ACTS Retreats and Missions.

Cyprian, St., Treatise IV on the Lord's Prayer, Description of Shadrach, Meshach and Abednego

Psalm 100:4   Didache Bible

All other Psalms   New American Bible/St. Joseph's Edition

Using Scripture Verses

Isaiah 55:11   New American Bible/St. Joseph's Edition

John 17:22-23   New American Bible/St. Joseph's Edition

Romans 8:28   New American Bible/St. Joseph's Edition

Jeremiah 29:11   New American Bible/St. Joseph's Edition

Over the Womb of a Pregnant Spouse and Praying Over the Children

MacNutt, F.; MacNutt, J., (1988) Praying For Your Unborn Child New York, NY: Doubleday.

Over Each Other

Philippians 4:6   New American Bible/St. Joseph's Edition

Matthew 11:28-30 New American Bible/St. Joseph's Edition

For Healing

Exodus 15:26   New American Bible/St. Joseph's Edition

Luke 9:1-2   New American Bible/St. Joseph's Edition

Healy, M., (2015) Healing: Bringing the Gift of God's Mercy to the World   Huntington, IN: Our Sunday Visitor Inc. (the four steps referred to in booklet are adapted from the five steps in Dr. Healy's book)

Intercessory Prayers

Romans 8:33-37   New American Bible/St. Joseph's Edition

James 5:17-18   New American Bible/St. Joseph's Edition

For Baptism in the Holy Spirit
Pope Emeritus Benedict XVI
"Let us discover, dear brothers and sisters, the beauty of being baptized in the Holy Spirit."   Pentecost 2008 Traditional Sunday Greeting: Zenit News Agency.

"A life transforming experience..."   ICCRS (International Catholic Charismatic Renewal Services) Doctrinal Commission; the National Service Committee of the Catholic Charismatic Renewal in the U.S. Inc.

Sheila's personal witness...

Magnificat (Canticle of Mary) Luke 1:46-55

John 14:6   New American Bible/St. Joseph's Edition

Acts 1:4-5   New American Bible/St. Joseph's Edition

Matthew 7:7 — New American Bible/St. Joseph's Edition

Psalm 37:4 — New American Bible/St. Joseph's Edition

(Lawrence, Br., 1958) The Practice of the Presence of God Old Tappan, NJ: Pyramid Publications.

Ephesians 6:18 — New American Bible/St. Joseph's Edition

Psalm 116:12-13 — New American Bible/St. Joseph's Edition

In Tongues

Acts 2:3-4 The Catholic Study Bible

1 Cor 14:39-40 — New International Version

Proverbs 3:5-6 — New American Bible/St. Joseph's Edition

Romans 8:26-27 — New American Bible/St. Joseph's Edition

Using Gifts of Knowledge and Prophecy

Jeremiah 31:3 — The Didache Bible

Matthew 28:20 — New American Bible/St. Joseph's Edition

Jeremiah 29:11 — New American Bible/St. Joseph's Edition

Spiritual Warfare Prayer

1 Timothy 6:12	The Didache Bible
Romans 8:37	The Didache Bible
Ephesians 6:11-12	The Catholic Study Bible
Ephesians 6:18	The Catholic Study Bible
Luke 11:4	The Catholic Study Bible
Matthew 18:21-22	The Catholic Study
1 Peter 4:8	The Catholic Study Bible
Matthew 4:1-11	The Catholic Study Bible
2 Timothy 1:7	The Catholic Study Bible
John 10:10	The Didache Bible

Contemplative Prayer

Luke 5:4	The Catholic Study Bible

Merton, T., (1972) New Seeds of Contemplation New York, NY: New Directions.

1 Samuel 3:9   The Catholic Study Bible

Various Other Types of Prayer

Pray More Novenas   www.praymorenovenas.com

Closing

"Be a saint! What else is there?" Patrick Coffin Catholic Radio

James 1:17   New International Version

1 Peter 4:10   (Paraphrase) "As generous distributors of God's manifold grace, put your gifts at the service of one another, each in the measure he has received."

Numbers 6:24-26   The Didache Bible

Back cover

Psalm 37:39   Responsorial psalm from Ordinary Time